I0558667

new words
{issue seven}

a trans* poetry journal

new words {press}
New York, NY
www.newwordspress.com | @newwordspress

new words {press} is a sponsored project of Fractured Atlas, a non-profit arts service organization. Our mission is to elevate emerging and established trans* and gender-expansive poetic voices, to build community, and share knowledge.

copyright 2025 © new words {press}
issue six

ISBN: 978-1-968528-03-4

Cover Design by brooklyn baggett
Photo by brooklyn baggett
Typesetting by new words {press}
Font: EB Garamond

{staff}

brooklyn baggett (she/her)
managing editor // bimbo

Lena Kassin (they/them)
co-editor // submissions manager

Lena Kassin is an editor at new words {press}. They hold a BA from Reed College and live in New York, where they were born and raised.

Jory Mickelson (they/them)
guest reader

Jory Mickelson is an award-winning transgender writer and educator living in Xwot'qom / Whatcom / Bellingham on the homelands of the Lummi and Nooksack peoples. They are the author of three books of poetry: Picturing (2025), All This Divide (2024), and Wilderness//Kingdom (2019) which won a 2020 High Plains Book Award. Their work has appeared in Prairie Schooner, Poetry Northwest DIAGRAM, Jubilat, and other journals in the US, Canada, and the UK.

Birch Wiley (he/they)
guest reader

Birch Wiley is a transsexual poet living in New York. Their work can be found in Pleiades, Voicemail Poems, and Querencia Quarterly, among others. Their debut collection, Mythweaver, was published by new words {press}.

griffin epstein (they/them)
guest reader

griffin epstein (they/them) is a settler working in education and community-driven research in Tsí Tkaròn:to (Dish with One Spoon/Treaty 13). They are the author of two chapbooks: "so we may be fed" (Frog Hollow Press, 2021) and "it matters how we live" (Black Sunflowers Press, 2026). griffin plays with the bands LOST UNIT and SPOILS and is a member of the Biophilia Collective. Their poetry has appeared in new words (press), CV2, Grain, Muzzle, Variant, The Maynard and Plenitude, among others. They believe in harm reduction, disability justice, and a free Palestine.

{table of contents}

Nino McQuown

Super Bowl Sunday and the Dove Did Not Come Down

I want to eat a heart-shaped pizza. I am still alive.
And to text all the drivers in Kansas City who told me where to go
for barbecue and what barbecue to eat. It was a kind town,
surprisingly, houses like jeweled birds, windows like the geometric carapace of
one humongous bug, or a fly's wing, I didn't look in. I saw only the outside.
Sorry
sorry, some asshole comes
to gather us like fishes everywhere we crowd for joy.

It doesn't even make the news, his pistol slipping like a minnow through us
unless there's a tie-in, or numbers, that's America: Two women
in team t-shirts looking scared
for their lives like they don't give a shit about football. Behind them
a train station where yesterday I stopped to see
the fountains running red.

Online in America they say while we were watching
the game the bombs were falling on Rafah. Snipers hang
in the teetering jaws of the city shooting anyone who moves. Coil in its empty
sockets snipering. A woman lies dead in the street over the body of her dead child whom
she came for. When we celebrate it is already in us, this touchdown

this good death this covering
the body of our own beloved sadness death for nothing,
death for free death for the price of a heart with a murmur, an unsteady, following
beat. Look, the day lays over
us like an annihilating star. Between Rafah and Kansas City

there is no one who can love you enough. All those wings, all those wings,
they kept saying, severed at the joint and the tips are especially delicious.
Anything could be a prayer at this point. There
is no one who could love you enough to save your life.
You should be happy to know the price of wings has gone down.

Ellery Liverseed
Greyhound

Outside, a man faps.
A lady takes a drag. Midwest sky and baby eyes
fly by the anti-drug/
BBQ billboard tells me to
Smoke brisket, not meth. Someone
screams for help. Someone
ties a shoe. Alone enough now to
prune my life down to a
single thorn: Original,
pervasive aloneness. Windows. Blurred trees. Stale cereal, cigarette
dirt coated floor. Weed bleeding
from his jacket pocket. Sweat and tin. Foreign
gray tone. Body of bird
littered sides. Eyes of
striped creatures still moving.
Cans they forgot. But I
know winning. It's
done from a confetti velvet
seat. Strange legs kicking
just enough to crawl. Lungs
cracking open
just enough to
fill with wind.

Kath Healing
Field Note with Animal Silence

the deer does not startle
when i name myself wrong.

her ears swivel,
not toward me—
but toward the crow
    counting my missteps in gravel.

i kneel.
the moss inhales
    what i cannot tell.
a root presses back—
    not refusal,
    not a spell,
just the memory of soil
    keeping records.

the creek stutters under stone.
i write: water = patient,
stone = witness,
body = misplaced species.

night arrives
without triage.

i do not check boxes.
i listen
    until the silence
        finds my lungs
            and starts breathing.

Sophie Dufresne
Six in(ter)dependent couplets

Ekphrasis of a (lost) memory:
The art of forgetting

Walking by Roasters BBQ at Alexis Nihon,
I almost see his reflection in the window.

Making eye contact with soldiers while wearing the keffiyeh,
Hoping they grow a conscience but knowing they won't.

Closure is overrated,
Not every wound requires stitches.

This unfinished skyline, threatening me with unfulfilled potential;
The pit in my stomach, a reminder of my own.

Stargazing near a soccer field,
I count three stars and two satellites.

Molothrus A.
an evolution of dysphoria hoodies

figure i (2014)
navy blue, grey sleeves, with a horizontal stripe around the cuff
provided as part of the subject's school uniform
on a classroom window, the subject scribbles notes
about brood parasite birds and resents
resents until their skin stings with envy
their ability to adapt, to disguise, to endure
to lie to their wardens from the time before their birth
the subject goes to detention for this
and sits in a room of navy blue and grey bodies
knowing she is simply in camouflage
and she does not belong to the nest
the subject's waist is obscured
the subject's chest is partially obscured

figure ii (2019)
all black, slightly cropped, with "forget" embroidered across the chest
the subject first wears it when stargazing with their father
who cannot read the embroidered foreign script
who no longer knows the subject's name
together, they try and fail to map the sky
and together, they laugh
while searching for Ursa Major in the wrong hemisphere
and in their father's face, the subject sees their own crooked lip
and shallow curve of the eye
which briefly renders the sky above them irrelevant
the subject's waist is obscured
the subject's chest is obscured
the subject's face is obscured

figure iii (2023)
canary yellow, with a small patch on the left wrist
that depicts two rabbits fornicating
the subject and his friends pile into a secondhand honda odyssey
and drive, from sunrise to a southern creek
some of his friends are subjects, just like him

he rolls down the window and sticks out an arm
fingers splayed, fucking rabbits fluttering in the wind
over and over, the odyssey's radio loses signal
and, missing every other line, the subject and his friends sing
a canary yellow song
the subject's waist is obscured
the subject's chest is obscured
the subject breathes, deeply and with no remorse

Veda Carmine-Ritchie

loop

I rode all the way home.

pulling rocks out of my hair,
crumb by crumb
bugs from fur
Snowflake extracted from the bank

It connects me to the
pieces of the whole

sweat on my bike seat, bleeding through belted layers
headed back from the boys club.

I shed half a pound of dead cells across the linoleum,
leaning back in my chair

Exchanging glances at the older man with the tight jeans
drip deli coffee on the piano. It's 6pm.

He smells of whiskey.
I am told I serve 'andro realness'.
It's Tuesday.

Jason puts one barrette on each side and it makes me giggle a little closer.
We put lipstick on and become two boys in the women's department, wanting ourselves.

Like a phone flashlight in a basement archive,
Naked in the dust I could fumble with the knob of your hip bone.

still, I know it's no matter,
I count my fingers and my toes while you go soft on me.

Tonight I'm on stage and my submission demands a song.
Call it trailer park swing –the stranger in cat ears hums along.

Bathing in the sweat on my way home,
I like the taste it puts in my mouth.
I belt layers around my waist and tuck my scarf behind my ears.

One headphone in, one headphone out.
I bleed through my briefs onto the seat, down to the pedal.

I push forward through the streets and wind behind, between.
I strain and coast. I bend laws and obey physics, I try to ease up
I continue moving away, knowing I'm bound to
circle home when all this is over, or maybe I'm already home and
I'm bound to
stray.

I learn how to adapt to the body I was given,
and align it with the cartoon character living in my forehead.
Gears click into place, and fall out, and click, and I am shifted and set on forward.
Unable to deny that I used to ask for you to

carry me,
carry me,
carry me.

Devin Fitzgerald
Where do you go after your second divorce?

i sway at the alter & black sequins wink
as drag Jesus' beard tickled my chin.
40 years, two marriages, loving women,
men & finding bits of life on the ground as
i fall into the Lord's eyes, pasties swirl
each one a galaxy of promises for tomorrow.
the demons in me sing & dance, grinding
noting i've only got three lovers in the room
the rest wanted to avoid hearing poems
since they are all about death or love or
listening to wind in trees like Mary Oliver.

                    boring shit
not about the sex parties
where by 3am i can't remember the mouth
or mouths i've seen with rubies inside.
when i wake up on the floor it seems from
the echoes of touches & peeling
laughs fading that we all got too busy alive
to remember how sour this beer will be.
the sticky floors are a gift to our memory
Just a quiet grip-hiss tugging at feet saying
'remember-forget, remember-forget'

barboring

how to be Annie and how to find someone like Beth while squirt-ing on flowers in the draught

first, acquire deep love for your favourite porn star
in colours and flashes and special effects, all sprinkled
then, realise it's named Annie

then, start sex work yourself,
in any form,
even if it's doing grassalingus in your garden,
asking earth to pay,
but actually, when they don't pay, understanding that you're the one in debt from a long
long time ago

then, find Beth
even if it was Beth that found Annie first
and make sure that Beth has a motorbike
forgive them if the only way they go is on a stick horse
mount together, and make the woods wet

for 3 nights and 3 days squirt on plants, flowers, trees, mountains
and everyone else in need
and then, lay down, play dead
feel yourself rot
together inside the earth so sexy and so hot

Christa Lei

triptych of golden disobedience

I.

my mother gripped my wrist and led me into the field. she never said why we had
to lie down, only that the ground would help me remember. wheat stalks brushed
against our calves as we sank into the soft loam. she whispered our lineage until
nyx appeared in her primordial essence. cloaked in dust and hush, her gaze vast
enough to tuck us in & swallow us whole.

selene stayed silent. further off, she watched guard, the glow of her lantern guiding
us back to sweet eleusius.

II.

i fucked up and fell.

not like there were options between the rotating pantheon of broads my father and poseidon
screwed and the rest of olympus fucking. i was bred from divine runoff, a mistake, an
afterthought. genetically convenient virginal princess of spring.
maybe mother's grip was too tight.
i pulled away. unraveled. fell through the cracks while hades played savior. when the moirai
found out, they did not flinch. they knew she'd waste years calling it an abduction.

but i was never lost, so how could i be found?

III.

we promised that we'd grow into the mythos we were writing—that palpable tension meant
chemistry, an initiation into stockholm syndrome disguised as crazed lust. on our wedding night,
he danced naked amidst scant luminescence. his fingertips reverent and unfamiliar, tracing my
curvature in broad strokes. i told myself it was love.
he serenaded me to the stylings of spandau ballet's gold while i twirled around him.
i dissolved into his arms.

he came once.

Elena Sichrovsky
Septum Piercing in Your Soul

Pyromania

Every time you have sex he fucks like it's the last time. You are constantly having *ten-minutes-after-breaking-up, leaving-for-a-two-month-business-trip, final-affair-between-two-best-friends* sex. The bedroom ceiling grows foggy, thick with a smoke from a fire that roars as abruptly as it smothers itself. The crescendo morphs into sorrow even before you go soft in his grip.

Every fuck is crackling popcorn under your skin, ferocious in the faith that tomorrow is never going to ring the doorbell. Every time it also involves him crying before / during / afterwards / combination of all three.

He worships you so intensely that you've come to resent being a god. You want to be kissing prayers across his skin instead of always the one receiving them.

Fibromyalgia

You don't know how to make him believe you. How to prove to him you aren't going to become a pumpkin at midnight; you aren't going to turn him back into a frog; your enmeshed limbs won't disintegrate into sea foam.

You say *Smell my bones and recognize your scent there. Read the stretch marks on my thighs and spell out our life after death. Pluck the taste buds from my tongue, each of the five deities I would slay to bring you back to me.*

He ejaculates too soon against your stomach, white filling the cave of your navel. His body coils around you like the turquoise hem of a bruise. He keeps an arm across your chest all night so that he can memorize the exact moment should you disappear and leave raw bed sheets beneath.

You inhale his snores like helium / pour shrill / i love yous / into his dreams.

Paraphernalia

You can't explain to people what you love most about him. They wouldn't understand why you adore that he wears ivory but never green. Why you love his strong opinions about bus stop signs. Why you love how his crooked wisdom tooth makes him bite the inside of his cheek and he still refuses to get it removed.

Don't chew on that side, you tell him, *or at least chew slowly.* Still at least three times a week while eating he'll pause / half-whimpering / half-grinning / shameful while crumbs spill and speckle his unshaven chin.

One night when he's sitting and eating a mandarin on the edge of the bed, he bites the inside of his cheek again. You reach over and run your thumb across his jaw, wiping the orange spill away. A gesture no more two seconds long, and somehow *that's* what finally does it. More than the hours of sex, more than your breath tattooed on his thighs, more than tracing *i exalt you* into the circumference of his tongue.

That night he asks to try fingering himself to prepare for penetration. You've never experimented with that type of foreplay, and there are a few beats of awkwardness at first, but it ends up being just as arousing as you'd hoped. You nibble at his tear-streaked cheek and tell him it's something you would love to do again.

"Maybe tomorrow," he mumbles, wet lips catching on your falling hair.

You freeze, hovering above him on your elbows, your chest swelling like a firmament about to crack.

Fuchsia

/this is how/ *You are sitting at the round oak table in the kitchen of your two-room apartment wearing polka-dot boxers and a blue velvet bathrobe. There's a pink flamingo ceramic plate in front of you loaded with a pile of scrambled eggs and three slices of buttered toast. A half empty jar of apricot jam sits next to the knife and fork. Your feet are socked and lying flat on the sand-colored floor tiles. The kitchen window is half open behind you and the fern from the garden outside is plastered against the rain-stained glass. The coffee machine beeps and you get up and refill your coffee mug, the one with little reindeer antlers on the handle. Then you reach across the table and fill his cup, too.* /our story begins/

Rainier McCall
missed connections: you were omniscient and intangible, I saw you in the clouds
[crossposted: rants and raves]

do you know if God will still love me? since I'm everywhere. in biohazard bins, flaming garnet, as they are. in trash cans, melting in the florida sun. in test tubes and vials; a clinic's fridge.

will God hate me because parts of me are gone? or replaced? inked over like an angry child's first journal?

was I selfish in my editing?

Is there a way to navigate the world without doing so? where does the line get drawn? it's okay to pierce ears, says Bible, says missionary, says mom. but not nose, not eyebrow?

was it impermissible to hold my ego above creation?

does heaven hold a space for me; the one who scattered myself like a demented version of a sharing of ashes across a battered beach?

if you have the answer, write me. I need to know.
[do NOT contact me with unsolicited services or offers]

Melinda Freudenberger
Summer in New York

over the bridge once again the shortness of time is impressed upon me as if god himself

has eased his blessed and oiled thumb to my forehead as if he is pushing, insistently,
    through the bone

amidst dreams of a sealed mouth dreams of a marriage with someone who doesn't love me

dreams of wandering the subway stations, lost, pulling

my body up flights of crooked stairs, knee aching till it nearly snaps—

i'm in a cab, then, the city in its haze of heat and shit while the driver talks of visitations

this is how you see the beauty of god, he holds my eyes in the rear view mirror,

the camera in my car is always pointing up toward the sky, he says and tilts it even higher

a grey glittering ufo dipping over a quiet empty highway

two angels, hovering at his bay window with a smile

i imagine the angels as bags of translucent skin, streaks of light, and from each crevice

a wing sprouts as if a seedling as easy as sun-slipped sweetness as good as it too—

the angels can feel the weight of my Looking upon them like a spirit

eyes begin to bloom, lids slide back to reveal wet pearls rolling like hard candy on a tongue

didn't god say we could not bear to see love like this so close? it is

Looking like need, like easy, like a hand at the nape of my neck

Looking like a kiss in the quiet, like a blue-robed madonna set serene in stone

god's centerfold of desire

alie rain davis

Becoming Particulate

after Oliver Baez Bendorf

There are days my body is only spirit-
bag; meat and bones stacked up
like a scooby-doo sandwich; red blood cells,
white. All of these fingers and toes and this
big fat tongue loose in my mouth. Not really sure
if the brain is weighed down a rock in a river
or if it's suspended like a fetus in aquatic

   bliss. The inner machinery stays in the dark
   in more ways than one. But my own irises
   I have observed lovingly: snakeskin color-
   shifting in the changing light. We have
   the same eyes our whole life, unlike almost
   everything else. Even our skin dies
   and is reborn on a cellular level. They say

      about every seven years your body is complete-
      ly made anew. What a blessing it is to be so meticulously
      resurrected. I ask the universe to be gentle with me
      for a little while. Give me time to make something
      from all of this discard: the hair I cut over
      the bathroom sink, the dust that gathers
      like a seam of my once-body. I've wept over it

         in an apartment where I lived to love someone
         else. When we left for good I showed them
         the grey of it on my finger and said, this was us—
         thought making dust of myself was a kind of loyalty
         to romance and watched as I crawled towards
         the definition of nothing, for which any kind of burial
         is impossible.

Magdalena Styś

two countries and counting

nobody moves like you 'round these parts. stagnant grass overflows, cars pass by parhelia, gears unchanged, the radio wailing in mores code. it's sterile and unsalted, it's cheap moonshine and investment banking and the recent overuse of the em-dash; it's *did you hear* and *don't you know* and never *let me lend you my eyes, let me unscrew my hands, let me show you how to make this shithole lovable.* do you still sleep in the bed we wrecked? on the bright side of this loneliness lives time to buy more nails, to polish the hammer and the amaranth, to soften the sheets. would you let me return, practice what you taught me?

alie rain davis

death to the bedframe I built for you / like a city I am remade

It's been a while since I was turned object
flattened with my legs sprawled open
built in a year over the corpse of another
I become one with the floor
I want everything to look real
my shit is getting rocked on my floor mattress
by a random bisexual man from a dating app
I don't tell him I took apart my bedframe
I hid all the pieces in my closet
happy as hell for a small sense of control
I stayed still and let myself get rearranged

I was made two-dimensional
like a neighborhood
bent like a piece of paper I said a body-prayer
for the particle board and wood veneers
the objects around me resemble nothing
every night I get disassembled
my dreams fall out in unrecognizable shapes
I scraped the skin off my foot
I did it all without instruction
I hung my bleeding foot off the side of my bed
and it stained the hardwood

Andie Brynn Weaver
At the End of the World,
I Drink the Candle

at the end of the world   I drink
the candle   feel the hot wax
pouring down   sealing me up
like the stamp of a king   my
throat is a pulsing automaton
my throat is a water wheel
pushing back small and searing
tides   I did not think I still had a
throat my throat is burning still
I do not stop   I drink the candle
and I know it tastes nothing like
it smelled   I know the candle
will not end   I know there is
enough to fill me forever   my
ears puff and crack like glass
forgotten on a burner   I did not
think I still had ears   the heat
shoots   like   campfire   sparks
behind my nose and eyes   I did
not think I still had a nose or eyes
in my chest   the flames carve a
cavity I couldn't feel before   I
did not think   I still had any of
these things.

Melinda Freudenberger
Fantasy

If I tell the truth will it let go   Of me? Like subway-window ringworm like
    the morning L train piss breeze—

The inconceivable sentence sits across from me in the dimly lit room Wholly and
    without fear

I kiss the unmentionable word so deeply it flattens the need for god

If I tell the truth will it   Will it wound me?

You, angel of limited time and endless sun, materialize under my sheer curtains palms-first

Our story is tired and long but I'll tell it anyway: you come from

Paradise, a place with no buildings no cars no rent and you take a body

All to lay two fingers in my mouth and watch them disappear between my lips

Heaven begins in the throat

Locked in cosmic situationship   The fantasy, if nothing else, is determined

Is striking in its mindlessness as it descends upon us like a dove

If I fuck the unnameable thing till my bed is cool and slick with sweat will it Heal me

It is so easy to be cruel in a poem

In this fantasy I am your blunt axe Your dry well

And you are the light which streams in through my windows just to tell me it   Loves me

To show me what I'm losing one last time

Micah Scheff
Mother

What does God say when he speaks to a shell of a shell: what grief makes of you? A giant, husking thing.
There is skin, formless, skull-soft, – with your blood, blue mirrors – and a chance to crawl inside while it's
still fresh. What an agonizing home you've made. We ridge against each other. You cut my bangs too short
and cry when I turn the corner.
Some call these 'growing pains'.
Why isn't your little girl your little girl anymore? Brainwashing – shaky cam foot-age of UFOs, the fluoride
in the water, the President, CIA, and Men in Black at Bohemian Grove – is a funny thing. It can happen to
anyone, even –
recluse spiders, gorging themselves on the flesh of nymphs.
There is an entire g –end–er between us and a refusal to vacate. Guiltless invader, what you seek is not
hidden inside, but I'm turned over anyway.
Caution: eat what you hate and it becomes you.
Chipped teeth and long nails.
Dyed hair, chemical in the free wind.
I am thinking of –
days long past.

Eel Probably

titleless, OR "The word you've entered isn't in the dictionary. Click on a spelling suggestion below or try again using the search bar above"[1]

THIRD ACT:the dead second, or (⟵○⟵)

documentation
        of an entity entombed:: in a technique described as

                the "photobiont-becoming-of-being-ness" (as Its called) of

                      a being that cannot bite sting fight run away it is classified as
        completely helpless

an exoskeleton is coming into emotion; an sharpened article of speech proposes to itself

the ↘*closer-to-death* non-caterpillar
forms the *butterfly that builds a house soon to be forgotten*

revelations tied once to **the ↘*closer-to-death*** non-caterpillar, hereby referred to as "*ITS*'ts"
ability to remember are dissolved by the (i)nhab(i)tants of the new form (((it is an embedding of
inherited inscriptions
not a vivisection thereof–)))

>the *ITS*'ts provides a feeling(*emotional state, a reaction*), of butterfly-becoming transforming
into:

SECOND TO LAST FIRST ACT:The End Angle: A Toggle State

      → sinking as if falling
      → a deepening of the fingers
      → a state of turning around and not crying
      → licking and peaking around and about oneself and/or others
      → being the first to lie about the butterfly

Let's get serious!
What is the future of the caterpillar, the will, or the detritus? ^
The *ITS*ts[dying caterpillar] is already the *ITS*ts[dead butterfly], and it is imperative that these
creatures
        become categorized

---

[1] go to this link if you don't believe me https://www.merriam-webster.com/dictionary/titleless

efficiently
using full *phrases* derived from the English *language*.

> 1
> 2
> 3
> 4
> nvm...

in a display case of 1x9ITS'ts.

1. find a butterfly (egg v.2) where thinking and dissimilation are the intensities of *CATASTROPHIC*-chrysalis-sleep, this occurs in the landscape of often-star space*[2],

Write your answer in the provided space:

_____

_____

_____

_____

_____

_____

DISRUPTive ACTION:performed by one or two or any number of *Homo sapiens* **that prevents the continuation of the story at all cost.**

the last things to ⤢ [ever exist] will be:

a scrap of paper, the feeling of mud ↖

as soon as the butterfly emerges, it is already singe-ING at the edges
releasing vibrant hues of illegibility (SO THANKFUL)

Conclusion! Congratulations! Collusion!

↕

- a worm of nonsense seeks the reliability of forms
- wrinkles
- bumps
- designs spotting and streaking [fugitive]
- turning itself in on an outing downtown, the cry-me-a-river crime:
  - "I realized I was myself."

_____

[2] 1,000,000,000,000,000,000,000,000 inhabitants

I.   the Cater Pillar Cat's Dog Hairy Cat submerges in the opalescent suspension here-
by <.rendingcrafting> itself into a stranger to itself from itself

diary entry catching fire just beyond the 16:9 screen ratio
april second, millennia # beyond counting

> *I woke*
> *up singing a softly shaking melody to myself.*
> *It went something like "Hmmmm... hm...*
> *hm-hm-hm... hm hmmmmm..." I realized*
> *that the ochre present had run out. I'm not*
> *who I ever thought myself to be, and that's*
> *really okay to me because beautiful bodies*
> *are starting to emerge all around and under*
> *the edges that I was told were to have been*
> *sealed.*

STAGE RIGHT: FIRST ACT, SCENE 180
;bu↵rning froth is reflecting in the mirror.
My eye catches the miracle and I wonder what other reality I caught a glimpse of this time.

okayyy... soooo, *hgthy7*
I text my friend in the middle of the night, I can't sleep.

> with all surety, a syringe called *denouement* siphons echoes from the vial of
> activity-processing-thinking that is called a **II.** chrysalis
> (((once a *golden sheath*)
> ((((((secondly a *case for a dormant being*(((((((
>))))thirdly in these days::::::::::::::::::::::::::::::::::;,,,,,,
> *a a prescient foreshadow of the future carapace*
> *carnage {c/0ttage)*   ——— \\ ———

You have done so well. You have proven that you are alive. You have endured perfectly. You have.

LLThe First Second Third Act in Which Everyone Cries and Says Nothing Like This Has Ever Been Portrayed So Beautifully or has Happened Before77

the]descendingvehicle murmurs:

> horror, gentle::unfurling
> — 'death-body-death-death-flesh-real-death is to the house as ablution and prayer
> ablution and ablution are to us and ____*ITS*'ts____,,,
> '1& the same'

Victoria Jamilé

Repression is the Death of the Soul

Kelsey L. Smoot

Notes of a Native Son, as Jenga
after James Baldwin

In my dreams, I am my father's		
pride,	wound,	boy,
a son, not-son—an imposter, wearing his		
face,	clothes,	patience,
and wielding the blade of his love like a birthright		
On earth,	In his living room,	And in his eyes,
I am the smallest I've ever been; I hide myself within myself,		
and	like my father,	I
dream myself a new self—		
searching for	my beauty,	finding only
undeniable proof that we are not so different		

Susie Whittaker

the first rebellion in history to justify itself with the argument that there was no air-conditioning during a heatwave

the condom machine broke. like a monk's cell subsidised dawn aftershaves a vitreous lull: fuel oil myrrhs lampedusa pleather: the oration of hammer on bauxite on scaffold: an oxidising transience rectilines the sonoran desert. disaffection becomes autarkic when purified by the sublimity of rejection. the taps closed. like a nun's surplice price-gouged high-noon colognes a varnished hush: bleach incenses polyester archeology: the aridity of bass on engine on populit: a smirking gloom convexes its sewage tracts & chicken coops. a utopia expectant of its own immanence without the creation myth of pleasure. she thinks about when she went to the library to read about the war on terror as an aesthetic production before realising that she had a hole in her shorts and needed to buy deodorant before eating dumplings with the leicester city fan with huge boobs who went to pride with the finnish church in rotherhithe and who taught her how to suck the bottom lip while kissing. the timetables dimmed. like a novice's hab-it deregulated sunset urinates a loquacious sulk: lager lacquers post-fordist monkey bars: the steeling of football on masonite on tear duct: a soft-eyed anxiety curvilineates exit-ramp oranges & motherboard junkyards. the fantasy of exile as a deterritorialised extraversion of interior time. the escalators stopped. like a sister's veil mortgaged dusk pisses a gossiping blueness: weed stuccoes just-in-time swings: the tolling of rhyme on lungs on solomit: a rusting patience concaves death strips and firewater checkpoints. fatalism immobilises material transcendence as a transferable future. she drifts through limehouse on an late august evening and the barbecue smoke and the emptied cans and the rave posters pasted under the bridges tell her that she has always been watching.

Maya Williams

A Cento for Mad Horse Theatre Company's The Legend of Georgia McBride

> *from The Legend of Georgia McBride by Matthew Lopez, "Lost and Found" by Matthew Lopez and Joe Tippett, "Heartbreak Hotel" by Elvis Presley, "It Could Happen to You" by Johnny Burke, "Padam Padam" by Henrie Alexandre Contet and Norbert Glanzberg, "Express Yourself" by Madonna, "This Can't be Love" by Natalie Cole, "Redneck Woman" by Gretchen Wilson, "Lucky" by Britney Spears, "Firework" by Katy Perry, "Happy Days Are Here Again" by Jack Yellen and Milton Ager, "Because of You" by Kelly Clarkson, "Money, Money, Money" by ABBA, "Love on Top" by Beyonce', "Burnin' Up" by Jessie J, "9 to 5" by Dolly Parton, "I Will Survive" by Gloria Gaynor, and "Man! I Feel Like a Woman!" by Shania Twain*

Because of you,
I never thought it'd be drag queens that save my ass.
You make things less scary.
We are in the same boat now, baby. Grab an oar!
Because of you,
I found a new place to dwell.
Comme si tout mon passé défilait (As if my past was parading)
I ain't never been the Barbie doll type,
yet here we are: a straight man in drag and a drag queen in hell.
This is too sweet to be loved.
I stumble in the kitchen.
Hot in the kitchen.
It's time for makeup. Perfect smile.
There's not a thing in this world so bad that can't be fixed with a little makeup.
You're wearing a dress for God's sake. Use it!
Come on, show 'em what you're worth.
For you see my darlings, life is a banquet.
Get a little outta line.
Fool around and have a ball.
Let's go out there with our tits up and our testicles tucked.
Keep an eye on spring.
Because of you,
You showed me what was possible.
We all get to escape together.
Happy days are here again.
As long as I know how to love, I know I'll stay alive.
You put my love on top
Your love is real.

A. Riel Regan

I. My Therapist Tells Me to Practice "I" Statements

I must remember I am capable of learning.
I hope you use the journal I gave you.
I hope you can't escape me. I hope you
know I can't escape you. I taste blood, but
I am devoted. I will drown you
in honey. I wish to hold your tongue. I
only meant that you're my muse. I think I
see things some other way. I'm afraid. I
am afraid we'll die apart. I am so
afraid we'll die a tragedy. I need
help. I am changing. I met the mountain.
I am not blaming you. I don't want to
be this kind of animal anymore.
I must remember you are capable of not forgiving.

Cindy Gao

the party city lady looks at me and goes "??? what."

Are you looking for:
☐ Women's costumes
☐ Men's costumes
☐ No teeth, just a kid disguised as a ghost, bony little knees
and ratty sneakers peeking out from a silken bedsheet. All teeth,
a mouth separated from its hunger, snapping and biting and gnawing
towards something solid. Or how about the concept of Impressionism? Oh,
to be the shifting of light, the idea of change, so difficult
they have to invent a whole new field of mathematics to deal with me.
A history out of fragments. A solitary knife against the skyline, cutting
neon red trails. A pale red cloak that's gone as soon as it arrives. Lace-up boots
hugging me close as I bleed impermanence. Some sorta...
glitchgirl? Some place where my two realities meet in a collision
of pixels, smash-cut frame-to-frame of me collapsing onto this alter-
ego, this person ??? both more and less real than who I am now. Yeah.
That's it. This Halloween I want to be the story I tell about myself.

Josephine Simple
My Botch

he guides your hand by the wrist and points the mirror you're holding right where you
don't want to look. "look, it's all just one hole." the thing was supposed to have been
an imitation, instead you got an abstraction. "just one hole." the holes you're used to
eating are mucosal and drip with the specificities of the women whose legs they cleave.
you could never be mucosal, said the woman who made your thing. you had asked her
if she could customize: you had dreamt of long inner lips that stick out like a dopey
dog's tongue "absolutely not." but it's not hers anymore it's your legs and your life that
has been cleft. a biome of trauma buds in the ravine:

burnt out friends/caretakers sessions of oral sex that do something for your heart and
nothing for your clit cry for help group texts edited cry for help group texts deleted cry
for help group texts four AM sobbing running halfway across the brooklyn bridge
lying down on the wood walkway in this new land, spotted by yeast, drying lube, and
caked ointments, a brook of tears trickles
now gushes.
Who needs mucous
when your whole body is wet,
and your heart bursts with the
ten thousand, two hundred, and eighty one
nerve endings your clitoris doesn't have?
The surgeons can give you a hole,
but it is you who makes nothing from nothing.

J. M. Chadwick
Orlando

Long bacon strips where
I ride in the little red
car, flat down the high
way sitting stout and sticky,
sweat punching me in the back.
(I'm a woman with
a woman's problems. I like
to be held in the
night and I like to feel the
deep feeling. A sludgy pang.)
When stopped for healthy
lunch, I perform the practiced
task of looking at
your face and eyes right there while
your family watches me.
(I am a creature
made of the most disturbed in
gredients. I smell
like a bag of shit. We go
to the beach and coarse pubic
hairwaves.)
It's warm unlike our
burning winter. We sleep on
the terrace in a
tent because there isn't room
for us in their apartment.
(Looking at trees I
wish I was that orgasmic
purge of sweet pinkness,
coming then killing myself
like a bee or another
beautiful,shortthing.)
I'm in a towel
dress, we naked walk home back
to your family.
Legs bare, you and me become

a bug feast. There's a growing
hairygirlinsideofme.
***

(I wish I was cherr
y blossom I wish I could
Pop then be ended.
Maybe I'm serious a
bout this I am I am. What
ifIjustrottedafterwedidit,whatifmycarcassdecomposedineverybody'shands.

Charlotte Poitras
vagina dentata[1]

interior / weaponized
terrible
fish//shaped
entrance
wrapped in folklore
and
gendered fear

a sharp concept
lodged
(between psychology and ritual)
in the soft tissue
of
myth-making

penetration becomes
confrontation
she is
a cave
with teeth

~~not metaphor~~
~~not hallucination~~
but a structure
of *resistance*

the hero removes
one tooth
and calls it *marriage*

steel jaws
in soft bodies
a blacksmith's solution

---

[1] this poem was created as a collage using words or groups of words from Wikipedia article of the same titles

(forge desire, insert blade)
obsidian dream
devours
immortality

boys
fear
the girl
with a mouth
down there

she bites back
not because she wants to
but because they keep
calling her
a story.

Ezra McConnor Serra
I need to tell my friends that grief is like swallowing light

The light is dragging us out to the street
stuffy with pollen and other versions of us.
We move so fast in the past
we've hardly had any time to arrive here;
and we're turning back already,
though all the things we saw on the way in
are now turned inside out as if ungloved.

To keep away from all this,
I run down the street but it's just more light,
more trees oxygenating the memory.
Most things are a little hopeless like this
but then again we have these bodies
which can't leave us,
which have things called pulses
and scarring and hemorrhage.

Caleb Simon
Bodies that do not defy categorisation (like ours do)

/ work /
cold water /
planes /
car /
cadavers /
emails addressed
to a name that no
longer exists / folkloric
records / the empty centre
of an   austere office
building / a good wine
an   expensive   red /
a wooden frame with
the nails   hanging
out /   thick
hair /   letters /
dead   deer /
the   book
that these
rules are
written in /
the group that
defines these rules

D. M. Hartshorn

Your father does not recognize your voice

Take this drug at the same time every day.

In women of childbearing age,
this medication should be started during their menstrual period.
in women of childbearing age this medication should be started.
If not, then they should have a negative pregnancy test before starting;
before starting this medication
have a negative pregnancy.

Take this drug at the same time every day.

If you become pregnant or think you may be pregnant
if you think or if you become
if you think
you may be pregnant, if you
tell your doctor
if you become
tell your doctor, right?
Tell your doctor right away.

Take this drug at the same time every day.

This medication must
This medication must not be used
not be used during pregnancy. It may
harm an unborn baby. Exposure to female fetuses may result.
Exposure to female fetuses may result in virilization
this medication must,
must not be used.

Take this drug at the same time every day.

Breast-feeding while using this drug is not recommended
Using this drug is not recommended, it is unknown
It is unknown if this drug passes into breast milk.
It may affect milk production and it may harm a nursing infant.
Consult your doctor before breast-feeding.
Infant, consult your doctor
before breast-feeding
it is unknown.

Take this drug at the same time every day.

You may have withdrawal symptoms
when you suddenly stop
suddenly stop using
when you suddenly stop using the drug
you may have withdrawal symptoms.

Take this drug at the same time every day.

If you are female, tell your doctor right away
tell your doctor
if you are female
right away if you have any serious side effects,
including: deepening of the voice,
hoarseness,
unusual hair growth,
deepening of the voice,
enlarged clitoris,
hoarseness,
irregular menstrual periods
tell your doctor right away.

Take this drug at the same time every day.

Remember that this medication has been prescribed because your doctor
has judged that the benefit to you is greater than the risk of side effects.

Take this drug at the same time every day.

Remember that this medication has been prescribed
because your doctor
because your doctor has judged
that the benefit to you
the benefit to you is greater than the risk
the risk of side effects
because your doctor
has judged
that the benefit to you is greater
than the risk.

Take this drug at the same time every day.

Sharing this medication is against the law.
This medication is against the law
sharing this
is against the law.

Take this drug at the same time every day.

It is important to prevent pregnancy while using this medication.
It is important
This medication may affect the sperm.
This medication may
it is important to prevent
prevent pregnancy while using
it is important
while using this medication
may affect the sperm.

Take this drug at the same time every day.

This medication is a female hormone.
You are not a woman.

Take this drug at the same time every day.

This medication is used in men.
You are not a man.

Take this drug at the same time every day.

These symptoms may last
These symptoms may last from weeks to months
from weeks to months

These symptoms may last from weeks to months.

Kath Healing
Discharge Summary

Patient: [redacted]
Date: [today]

Chief Complaint
body keeps twitching
    under hospital cotton.

chart reads: persistent.
mouth reads: *untranslatable hum.*

History of Present Illness
Day 1: admitted for dissociation—
    diagnosis: metastatic glow,
        a shimmer too bright
        for charting.

Day 2: notes
    thunder has no gender.

Day 3: receives 0.5 mg
    of *animal memory*—
    tremor pauses,
        then blooms.

Day 4: scribbles on the consent form:
    "quiet doesn't protect me."
        [staff note: torn corner withheld.]

Physical Exam
- Reflex: moss rising
                between ribs.
- Pupils: respond
                to absence.
- Skin: holds a myth
                long after its burning.
- Speech: compliant affect,
                voice fractures mid-syllable.
- Sex: [not assessed]

Assessment
non-compliance
        with collapse.

relapse
        of breath
                into prayer.

multiplicity
        not supported
                in this facility.

Plan
                ·   discharge into field notes,
                                equipped with two lungs:
                                                one to breathe away,
                                                one to listen
                                                                for misnamed animals.
                ·   follow-up recommended
                                when patient no longer recognizes
                                herself
                                in broken maps.

Signature
voice flickers—

        computerized imprint,
                not closed,
                not clothed.

Jack Anthony

You're not non-binary. You're 26

I am not a man's man, ask any Bunnings[1] employee.
Trans women on YouTube taught me to shave.
                                    & on the rare days I exude masculinity,
                        it was practised and plagiarised
from the middle-aged butches
                        in a library book on queer history.

Not masculine enough
to hang with the boys,

                                                just masculine enough
                                            to get fucked by them.
                            Clearly clocked in women's spaces,
                                                            threat
                    made null
by a limp wrist
and considered comment:
                "I love your dress! It has pockets?!"

                            My friends
(all women)
                        say I'm a "girl's man"
Not a "lady's man"—
                        there is a difference.

                                            There is clearly
                                                a difference.

Advice to a baby dyke in a past life,
perceived predator of the
lady's locker room,

                                        even the patchiest
                                        beard can make
                a difference.
Go from sex pest
        to sexless
                    in just 2 years!

_____

1 Bunnings is an Australian hardware/home & garden store

Other side effects may include:
Failure to perform either binary,
A bank account drained by
hormones and surgeries that

                                               make and

displace me.

                 Inconveniencing GPs
            as a vague medical anomaly.

I do not feel like
a human being,

                                       so much as
                               a human trying—
             clinically, in community,
                 always

Advocating   or   Avoiding.
                 Identity as a

                                 euphoric

leaching

             act of creation,
             hovers,

hesitantly   wistfully
       between a rolled-up sock & the womb.
        I take comfort in the knowledge
          that, if I am nothing else,
              I am

                             the hottest man

in the
gynaecologist's waiting room.

Caleb Simon

To the magpie on the train tracks and me, coming out again

Lemon-zest legs shaking, as you teeter
somewhere between flight and flattened.
The days are long now
and all of them seem to be absorbed
by the trembling mass of your body,
wearing the turned-off light like a nightgown.

The train will arrive again
hurtling like the dam that keeps dawn's mouth jammed closed
has been wrenched open.
The train will arrive again,
and you will hop out of the way, again,

only to return to the tracks
in the only glowing spot of sun.

Ellery Liverseed
CAT

Television lit
sunset left rotting
in the sky like
forgotten produce drawer
mush. Stewed brown bled through
the thin fabric of
the fridge. My pants
her secret, the closed
door an angel and
the body that lays outside
it small, gray and
striped. Opened her mouth to scream and
swallow. And everything
she knows is everything I forgot:

How to flee and
let sounds out from
between your teeth

Shona Raine

A public commentary on the unholy art of bathroom melancholia: Resisting the mythologically sacrosanct design of binary space and social order

I pissed, unashamed, onto the grass.

Sebyul Paik

2023 *Texas Legislative Session Transgender Asian-American Blues*

The world is ending and it's Thursday evening.
I set my phone face-down on the counter and focus
On making dinner. Try to blink back the tears
As I chop onions. Not sure what I'm doing
With them yet. I wipe my eyes with my sleeve
But it doesn't help much. The world is ending
And I've got a pot of water going on the stove.
We're making curry. You grumble about politics
While peeling the carrots. Those folks in Austin
Can't ever just mind their damn business, huh?
I nod along while checking the rice cooker.
The world is ending and I can't be bothered
To peel all these potatoes. You tell me it's okay.
Just scrub the dirt off. More nutrients that way.
Last week a stranger came up to me and told me
I was going to hell but he was praying for me.
I wonder if he's heard the news. If he's happy that
The world is ending and we're counting down
The days 'til we can get out of state. I scroll through
Zillow while we wait on the food. You ooh and ahh
At built-in bookshelves we can't never afford.
Neither of us really want to move but
The world is ending. Does anyone know
Where the ladle is? I keep meaning to buy another.
My mom gave me this one when I moved out.
Neither of us talk to our parents much
These days. I wonder if my folks even care that
The world is ending and we're settling down
In front of the TV to eat, because we're adults
And we can do whatever the fuck we want. We split
A soda because you know I can't finish a whole
Can by myself. The curry would be better with kimchi
But we're out because I never got around to going
To H Mart like I said I would last week and now—
The world is ending. The world is ending.

It's pretty good anyway.

Shona Raine

A treatise on flagrant workplace hysteria: Guerrilla art rejecting Timothy's cis-het patriarchal governance over the femme body

I shit my womb onto his desk.

Tess Ezzy
After the Fall

They think the myth ends with water,
with wreckage.
They never imagine
what happens next.

Icara stands on the shore,
seaweed tangled in her hair,
salt cut into her lips.
Alive, scarred,
yet shimmering.

The fall was not failure,
it was the undoing of every chain
that ever bound her.

She walks inland,
skin patterned with burn and tide,
the body remade
in its own language.

Not boy,
not warning,
not mistake.
A girl who flew,
and survived.

Wednesdae Reim Ifrach
Ritual of the Unbinary Body

gender is a house
   I refused to rent.
     I lit the foundation
       and danced in the smoke.

they still try to mail me
womanhood in government envelopes —
   I return them
     stamped:

body no longer at this address.

the moon calls me
by a name with no vowels —
only teeth
   and shadow
     and ink.

I am stitched with pigment,
a canvas uncompliant.
every needle a hymn,
every scar a shrine.

I do not transition.
   I transmute.
I do not pass.
   I possess.

and when I bleed,
   it is not prophecy
     but protest:

the body insisting
on its own wild grammar.

Nino McQuown

I Want the Ghost of Mary Oliver to Come and Slash my Tires

And I want you to be honest with me:

Is this animal soft? Or do I always

shake like this? If you're cold I'm cold,
let me in. My baby knows how to live. It struggles

and it loves what it loves until it's sleepy. Then
let's sleep. It's awfully compelling in Autumn.

We have a grey day and we'll be out here all year.
Almost every single leaf is falling is going to fall

is going to turn brown from this—whatever it is—Big
noise that happens all the time which is an argument

against evolution for utility since we aren't even the same
soft kingdom. Train me. I'm easy. I just want

fireworks for a few weeks. I like a long season in the
shoulders and a short one in the meat. The hot and cold

a whole transition with a middle of its own. All full of geese going
this way and that. I'm saying the trees aren't dying, they've just gotten tired.

We're doing what we love. We're getting jealous. All this beauty and
all this decay and they can do it and

undo it for centuries if no one cuts them down. If nobody
insists. In winter a tree is most alive in the trunk.

It's sugars drawn into that center chest for next
time's tender leafies. I used to be softer. In further

contrast to the trees, the dirt sucked something permanent
out of the backs of my hands. Now when she touches

me October through April she asks me what happened
to my knuckles. I have to say I held them too long unprotected

in the gardens of our adversaries. Rich
men in Washington and their rich wives who barely enjoy their own
lush patios. That's incidental though, all soil is thirsty, even poor soil that's what
leaves are for. But in this version of the timeline it was me

the earth had access to. It was my place to be eaten and I also raked
the leaves. I admit it. So the blameless dogs of our oppressors

could run around and piss. Rough work. Scored by fine minerals'
hard edges. Skin like a leaf in winter. Summers

I'm as bluff and fair of knuckle as a girl could wish against.
And tell me what it's like, being family with me and what

you want from your knees and when the end is coming
and will the end come again and again.

{contributors}

A. Riel Regan is a queer, emerging author with an intense appreciation for "the human heart in conflict" (Faulkner). Their writing often deals with conflict within the self, chronic illness, and knowing oneself through nature. Their poetry has been featured in Pine Mountain Sand & Gravel, Impossible Task, and Pegasus.

alie rain davis is a queer, nonbinary poet currently working towards their MFA in poetry at North Carolina State University. They have been published in Three River Review, Beast Grrl and Dragonfly Arts Magazine. alie has been involved with community workshops for ten years and believes another world is possible.

Andie Brynn Weaver is a queer nonbinary writer currently living in Lewiston, Maine. Their work can be found in new words {press}, Poetry South, The Rumen, and others. When they are not writing poetry, they are studying to become an archivist, pointing at birds, and trying to interpret their dreams.

barboring is a sex worker who likes pancakes, has issues with anxiety, SWERF and toilet flush.

Caleb Simon is a queer poet and maths student who can be found skulking about at open mics in Bath or empty fields in Worcestershire. Some of his work can be found in Fruit Journal, And Other Poems and Propel Magazine.

Charlotte Poitras is a neurodivergent and queer artist-entrepreneur based in Montreal, Quebec, Canada. She explores the blurred lines between fiction and reality through writing, visual arts, and short films with more than eighty publications. Her work aims to entertain both hearts and minds by embracing devil's advocate perspectives.

Christa Lei (they/them) used to be a professional astrologer and hopes you won't hold that against them. Their work appears in HerStry, Beyond Queer Words and Vast Chasm, amongst others. They live with their spouse and two dogs in New York City.

Cindy Gao (they/them) has poems in fifth wheel press, Eunoia Review, and the Oakland Review. They can be found thinking about time loops, failing at social deduction games, and working towards their degrees in Creative Writing and Behavioral Economics.

Devin Fitzgerald is a curator, librarian, nonbinary human from earth (allegedly). They organize poetry readings in Los Angeles. They are a member of the Burksy Collective.

D. M. Hartshorn is an astronomer making their home in Western Massachusetts. His poems can be found in Thimble Lit Mag, Mount Holyoke Review, Qu Literary, and elsewhere. They enjoy hot coffee in the summer, used bookstores, and the hunt for the perfect bagel.

Eel Probably identifies as a Disabled Queer Agender writer who creates work in a variety of genres, including but not limited to: fiction, poetry, essay, and experimental writing. Eel will be starting an MFA in Creative Writing this fall.

Elena Sichrovsky (she/they/it) is a queer disabled writer and cult survivor. Its work often explores trauma, grief, and identity through the lens of body horror. Their debut poetry chapbook "Eating Out Anne Sexton" was published in 2023 (Ghost City Press).

Ellery Liverseed is a queer writer, artist, and student. Their work has been previously published in Sink Hollow.

Ezra McConnor Serra is a queer Catalonian poet and zine artist in recovery based in Ireland who can be found cloud-gazing somewhere. They write about childhood, grief, addiction, anything akin to love, and individual/collective closeness to death. His work is fundamentally somatic but often entertains the abstract. They've been published or are upcoming in The Ex-Puritan, Archer Magazine, Seedlings, Verdict Magazine, Broken Antler Magazine, and Lucky Jefferson and he was a finalist in the latter's 2024 Poetry Contest. He's currently a reader for Palette Poetry.

J. M. Chadwick is a poet located in Manhattan. They were the 2023 recipient of the Ruth Forbes Eliot Poetry Prize. They love their wife, ducks, libraries, and making magnets out of cool buttons.

Jack Anthony is a writer and editor from Magandjin/Brisbane, Australia. His work has been featured in publications such as Querencia Quarterly, Ink & Inclusion, and #Enbylife Journal, among others. When not writing they can be found with their nose in a book, haunting op shops and bothering their cat, Jesper.

Josephine Simple is a writer, performer, and transsexual dyke based in Brooklyn. Her shows weave together comedy, dance, and Zen practice. Her writing has appeared in The New Yorker, Slate, and Poetry International.

Kath Healing (they/them) is a trans, non-binary, disabled, and neurodivergent poet living on the unceded territories of the Lək'ʷəŋən-speaking peoples (Victoria, BC). Their work explores myth, memory, and survival through queer embodiment and ecology. A single parent to two teens and three cats, they write toward survival and possibility.

Dr. Kelsey L. Smoot (they/he/Kelz) is a the author of two chapbooks: we was bois together with CLASH! (An Imprint of Mouthfeel Press) and Muse, with Another New Calligraphy. Thrillingly, Kelz's debut full-length collection of poems, SOULMATE AS A VERB arrives in early 2026 with DOPAMINE/Semiotext(e).

Magdalena Styś is a writer currently residing in Amsterdam. Their work has previously appeared in Moonday Magazine, Also Cool Magazine, and elsewhere. They were nominated to appear in the 2025 Best of the Net anthology.

Maya Williams (ey/they/she) is a religious Black multiracial nonbinary suicide survivor who served as Portland, ME's seventh poet laureate for a July 2021 to July 2024 term.

Melinda Freudenberger graduated from The New School with their MFA in Poetry in 2020. Their work has appeared most recently in Anomaly, Always Crashing magazine, and Spectra Poets. Their first chapbook, Dog Woman, is forthcoming from Harbor Editions in April 2026.

Micah Scheff (he/they) is a queer, Californian poet.

Molothrus A. can be found @molothrus.bksy.social.

Nino McQuown is a trans (and transdisciplinary) artist from Baltimore, Maryland, where they put on puppet shows, teach gardening, and make a podcast called Queers at the End of the World. They've published poems, essays, and comics with Foglifter, Edge Effects, Epiphany, Electric Literature, Barrelhouse, Cimarron Review, and others.

Rainier McCall (he/they) is a Florida born autistic abolitionist, Mad Pride advocate, survivor, therapist, and poet. Rainier is featured in anthologies, including a Lambda Literary finalist. Rainier can often be found verbally stimming to dad rock, curating odds and ends from the Y2K period, and reading esoteric Florida literature.

Sebyul Paik (they/them) is a lover and a hater in equal parts. They were born in California, raised in Texas and currently reside in Denver, Colorado. They studied Literature at the University of Texas at Dallas.

Shona Raine is a genderqueer poet exploring identity, language, and memory. Their work blurs form and function, mixing playful lyrics with reflective prose and visual art. Their poetry navigates social absurdities, liminal spaces and ancestral healing, transforming the intimate and forbidden into joy and rebellion.

Sophie Dufresne (he/they) studies creative writing at Concordia University in Tio'tia:ke/Montreal, Canada. He is interested in the way form informs content (or is it the other way around?). He is currently the copy editor of The Encore Poetry Project, a local literary and arts initiative.

Tess Ezzy is a poet, fibre artist, and researcher exploring the intersections of language, ecology, and emotional life. She founded The Moody Project, a studio transforming moods into art and poetry, and is completing a Master of Arts at UNE on ecological weathering in YA fiction.

Susie Whittaker (she/they) is a queer Marxist writer of poems from South London. She is currently influenced by E-40's Revenue Retrievin': Graveyard Shift and the novels of Mathias Enard, and has appeared in Passion of the Weiss, Impossible Archetype, Ouch! Collective, and Antiphony among others.

Veda Carmine-Ritchie is a writer and social worker living in Brooklyn, New York. They are the co-founder and literary editor for SplashLand Magazine. They have released two chapbooks Glossary of 82+ Dog Training Terms A-Z. (SplashLand, 2024.) and Rolodex (BottleCap Press, 2025.)

Victoria Jamilé (they/them) is a writer, collage artist, and lesbian goth born in Río Piedras, Puerto Rico. Utilizing horror, fantasy and nostalgia; Hernández writes/creates art about being a disabled femme-queer under a colonial power. Hernandez has been published in Fruitslice (2025), The Caribbean Writer (2025) and Latino Book Review (2025).

Wednesdae Reim Ifrach is a GenderQueer expressive art therapist, researcher, and poet whose interdisciplinary practice bridges clinical, creative, and community-based modalities. Their work culminates their training, artistry, and existential dread as a space where words and imagery emerge with the hope of helping others feel deeper.

www.ingramcontent.com/pod-product-compliance
Lightning Source LLC
Chambersburg PA
CBHW051334120626
46547CB00016B/2532